# SACRED STONES

**PHOTOGRAPHS BY**
**MICK SHARP & JEAN WILLIAMSON**

**A BOOK OF POSTCARDS**

*Pomegranate*

SAN FRANCISCO

Pomegranate Communications, Inc.
Box 6099
Rohnert Park, CA 94927
www.pomegranate.com

Pomegranate Europe Ltd.
Fullbridge House, Fullbridge
Maldon, Essex CM9 4LE
England

ISBN 0-7649-1037-X
Pomegranate Catalog No. A975

Photographs © 1999 Mick Sharp and Jean Williamson

Pomegranate publishes books of
postcards on a wide range of subjects.
Please write to the publisher for more information.

Designed by Barbara Derringer
Printed in Hong Kong
08 07 06 05 04 03 02 01 00 99   10 9 8 7 6 5 4 3 2 1

To facilitate detachment of the postcards from this book, fold each card along its perforation line before tearing.

**M**egalithic (very large stone) structures of a religious or ceremonial nature are found widely scattered across Europe. Most were built 3,000 to 6,000 years ago, in the periods classified by archaeologists as the Neolithic or New Stone Age (c. 4400–2500 BC) and the Bronze Age (c. 2500–1000 BC). The earliest megalithic monuments were chambers for communal burial, originally covered by long or circular cairns, or mounds of earth and turf. The more elaborate chambers were also used as sacred buildings, ritually entered and resealed at certain periods, with ceremonies held outside their impressive entrances. Many were oriented toward astronomical events; a few were constructed to allow the rays of the rising (Newgrange, Co. Meath, Ireland) or setting (Maes Howe, Orkney, Scotland) sun to pierce the passage and inner vault at midwinter. The burial remains—predominantly skulls and long bones—were often sorted and rearranged, and sometimes removed for use at other ceremonial centers. Archaeologists believe that some sort of ancestor worship was being practiced, and the excavated bones reveal that bodies were defleshed and exposed in the open air before being deposited in the chambers.

Next came the ceremonial earthwork enclosures (henges) and the large open rings of standing stones with outlying monoliths (single stones). Rings and other arrangements of stones were often placed within the encircling bank and ditch of a henge, and tree trunks were used as well as or instead of large stones. Stone rings of varying sizes and design were also erected without earthworks; the smaller ones and isolated single standing stones generally date from the Bronze Age.

# SACRED STONES

PHOTOGRAPHS BY
MICK SHARP & JEAN WILLIAMSON

### Men an Tol, Madron, Cornwall, England

The date and original form of this setting are unknown, although the carved stone resembles a small circular entrance to a Neolithic tomb. Children with rickets were passed through the hole three times; crawling through "nine times against the sun" put an end to shivering fevers. The movement of brass pins placed crosswise on the stone acted as divinators.

BOX 6099, ROHNERT PARK, CA 94927

Pomegranate

# SACRED STONES PHOTOGRAPHS BY
## MICK SHARP & JEAN WILLIAMSON

***Machrie Moor Stone Circles II and III, Arran, Scotland***
The surviving red sandstone pillar of Circle III has smooth
flanks and a weathered head standing over thirteen feet
above the ground. Broken stumps mark the rest of the
egg-shaped ring, which enclosed two cists containing
human bones, flint flakes, and a Bronze Age urn.

BOX 6099, ROHNERT PARK, CA 94927

Pomegranate

# SACRED STONES PHOTOGRAPHS BY
## MICK SHARP & JEAN WILLIAMSON

### Mid Clyth Stone Rows, Caithness, Scotland

Justifiably known as the Hill o' Many Stanes, the south-facing slope, with views to the sea horizon, is covered by about two hundred small stones. Arranged in at least twenty-two rows, they fan out north to south toward the lower end. Roughly six hundred stones made up the original symmetrical pattern, possibly forming a grid for Bronze Age lunar and stellar observations.

BOX 6099, ROHNERT PARK, CA 94927

Pomegranate

# SACRED STONES PHOTOGRAPHS BY
## MICK SHARP & JEAN WILLIAMSON

*Mabesgate, St. Ishmael's, Pembrokeshire, Wales*

Pembrokeshire's tallest standing stone, the Long Stone west of Milford Haven is believed to mark a Bronze Age burial. The moon shows itself over the horizon as the setting sun illuminates a stubble field.

BOX 6099, ROHNERT PARK, CA 94927

Pomegranate

# SACRED STONES PHOTOGRAPHS BY
## MICK SHARP & JEAN WILLIAMSON

### *Arbor Low, Middleton, Derbyshire, England*

This upland henge had an oval bank 250 feet across, created with limestone dug from the ditch. Causeways led to a central platform from entrances at the southeast and northwest, aligned with the positions of the sun and full moon at the solstices. More than forty slabs obtained from weathered limestone pavement were originally placed upright in an egg-shaped ring.

BOX 6099, ROHNERT PARK, CA 94927

Pomegranate

# SACRED STONES PHOTOGRAPHS BY
## MICK SHARP & JEAN WILLIAMSON

**Kingston Russell Stone Circle, Abbotsbury, Dorset, England**

Fallen stones now appear stranded in a field of maize; they once stood upright in an oval about eighty feet across. The axis of this Bronze Age monument was north to south; the eighteen stones gradually increase in height toward the north.

Pomegranate  BOX 6099, ROHNERT PARK, CA 94927

# SACRED STONES PHOTOGRAPHS BY
## MICK SHARP & JEAN WILLIAMSON

**Pentre Ifan Burial Chamber, Newport, Pembrokeshire, Wales**
Beneath a rising moon, the stones of a Neolithic chambered tomb
bask in the afterglow of sunset. Small stones on the left mark the
former extent of its long mound, constructed around 3300 BC.

BOX 6099, ROHNERT PARK, CA 94927

Pomegranate

# SACRED STONES PHOTOGRAPHS BY
## MICK SHARP & JEAN WILLIAMSON

### Lundin Links, Largo Bay, Fife, Scotland

These tall sculptural stones may have been erected in the second
millennium BC to record movements of the moon. A fourth stone
survived into the eighteenth century. Local traditions declare them
to be Druidic, Roman, or the memorials of Danish chiefs killed in
battle against Macbeth. Excavations beneath the stones in the
1700s unearthed coffins containing human remains.

BOX 6099, ROHNERT PARK, CA 94927

Pomegranate

# SACRED STONES PHOTOGRAPHS BY
## MICK SHARP & JEAN WILLIAMSON

### *Llech Idris, Trawsfynydd, Gwynedd, Wales*

Legendary giant Idris Gawr reputedly hurled this stone from his
chair on the summit of Cadair Idris, ten miles distant. Remote in
its upland setting, the stone dates back to the second millennium
BC. It apparently marked a Bronze Age track that headed inland
from the Llandedr coast and was associated with metal
prospecting and trading.

BOX 6099, ROHNERT PARK, CA 94927

Pomegranate

# SACRED STONES PHOTOGRAPHS BY
## MICK SHARP & JEAN WILLIAMSON

**Castlerigg Stone Circle, Keswick, Cumbria, England**
A storm flings shadows across the entrance portals of the
Keswick Carles. Set in a natural amphitheater high in the Lake
District hills, the large open circle of natural boulders is one of
the earliest in Britain. Ceremonies conducted there might have
included calendar celebrations, funerary rites, circular dancing,
and rituals associated with a stone-ax cult and with trading.

BOX 6099, ROHNERT PARK, CA 94927

Pomegranate

# SACRED STONES PHOTOGRAPHS BY
## MICK SHARP & JEAN WILLIAMSON

**Ballochroy Standing Stones, Kintyre, Argyll, Scotland**

The flat (right-hand) face of the central stone is aligned northwest toward the steep northern slope of sharply peaked Corra Beinn, one of the Paps of Jura, nearly twenty miles away. Currently the midsummer sun descends into a U-shaped gap to the south of the peak, but the stone accurately indicates the setting sun's position around 1800 BC.

BOX 6099, ROHNERT PARK, CA 94927

Pomegranate

# SACRED STONES PHOTOGRAPHS BY
## MICK SHARP & JEAN WILLIAMSON

### Arthur's Stone, Gower, Swansea, Wales

According to legend, King Arthur, finding this twenty-five-ton glacial erratic of millstone grit in his shoe, threw it seven miles, where it landed on Cefn Bryn Common. He split the stone with Excalibur, and still appears at full moon to admire his handiwork. Two prehistoric burial compartments and a holy well lie beneath the capstone.

BOX 6099, ROHNERT PARK, CA 94927

Pomegranate

# SACRED STONES PHOTOGRAPHS BY
## MICK SHARP & JEAN WILLIAMSON

**Torhouse Stone Circle, Wigtown, Dumfries
and Galloway, Scotland**

This well-preserved Bronze Age monument consists of nineteen
granite boulders arranged around the edge of an artificial platform.
The stones increase in height toward the shallower southeastern
arc. Near the center are the remains of a cairn, and three stones
aligned southwest to northeast. A lone monolith stands to the
south, another group of three stones to the east.

BOX 6099, ROHNERT PARK, CA 94927

Pomegranate

# SACRED STONES

**PHOTOGRAPHS BY MICK SHARP & JEAN WILLIAMSON**

### Northeast Circle, Stanton Drew, Bath and Somerset, England

Two ruined avenues and three stone circles occupy sheltered pastureland beside the River Chew. The complex is called the Weddings, after a party that recklessly celebrated into the early hours of a Sunday morning. Recent magnetic survey work inside the central circle—second in size only to Avebury—reveals nine concentric circles of holes thought to have held massive wooden posts.

BOX 6099, ROHNERT PARK, CA 94927

Pomegranate

# SACRED STONES PHOTOGRAPHS BY
## MICK SHARP & JEAN WILLIAMSON

### Ring of Brodgar, Orkney Mainland, Scotland

The Comet Stone southeast of the Ring is part of a remarkable
group of Neolithic ceremonial monuments positioned on land
separating Lochs Harray and Stenness. Inside a henge with two
entrances and a rock-cut ditch, sixty equally spaced slabs stood
in a true circle 340 feet across, forming a perfect foil to the
immensity of water and sky.

Pomegranate BOX 6099, ROHNERT PARK, CA 94927

# SACRED STONES PHOTOGRAPHS BY
## MICK SHARP & JEAN WILLIAMSON

### Clava Cairns, Inverness, Highland, Scotland

A ring-cairn, encircled by nine standing stones, forms part of
an extensive cemetery in use around four thousand years ago.
Four low banks of rubble create rays or spokes linking individual
uprights to the doughnut-shaped cairn. The passages of two adjacent
chambered cairns face southwest to the midwinter solstice sunset.
The three burial monuments form a northeast-to-southwest line
along a gravel terrace south of the River Nairn.

BOX 6099, ROHNERT PARK, CA 94927

Pomegranate

# SACRED STONES PHOTOGRAPHS BY
## MICK SHARP & JEAN WILLIAMSON

### *Adam and Eve, Avebury, Wiltshire, England*

Twin stone rows line processional avenues snaking away from the
huge Neolithic temple complex at Avebury. These two stones,
southwest of the main circle-henge, were once a part of
Beckhampton Avenue, toppled and buried in medieval times. Adam
formed the eastern wall of a boxlike stone structure, open to the
southeast; Eve stood as a pillar in the avenue's northern row.

BOX 6099, ROHNERT PARK, CA 94927

Pomegranate

# SACRED STONES PHOTOGRAPHS BY
## MICK SHARP & JEAN WILLIAMSON

### The Grey Mare and Her Colts, Long Bredy, Dorset, England

The burial chamber and curving entrance façade of a charmingly
named Neolithic long barrow. Mother and offspring stand on a
hill in farmland above Abbotsbury and the south coast.

Pomegranate

BOX 6099, ROHNERT PARK, CA 94927

# SACRED STONES

PHOTOGRAPHS BY
MICK SHARP & JEAN WILLIAMSON

**Ballochroy Standing Stones and Cist, Kintyre, Argyll, Scotland**

The stone row and exposed megalithic cist are in a line northeast to southwest, pointing toward Cara Island, a point where the midwinter sun would have been seen to set in 1800 BC. The view was blocked by a large cairn formerly covering the burial, but the initial alignment may have had symbolic value.

BOX 6099, ROHNERT PARK, CA 94927

Pomegranate

# SACRED STONES PHOTOGRAPHS BY
## MICK SHARP & JEAN WILLIAMSON

### Stonehenge, Amesbury, Wiltshire, England

Stonehenge probably evolved from a Neolithic sepulchre to a
Bronze Age sun temple. Before 3000 BC, a timber structure and
fifty-six pits containing cremated human bones lay encircled by an
earthen henge that faced the midwinter full moonrise. By 2000 BC,
the main alignment was to the midsummer sunrise, and unique
trilithons had been constructed of sarsen stones dragged from
the Marlborough Downs.

BOX 6099, ROHNERT PARK, CA 94927

Pomegranate

# SACRED STONES PHOTOGRAPHS BY
## MICK SHARP & JEAN WILLIAMSON

**Trethevy Quoit, St. Cleer, Cornwall, England**

A rectangular stone box, Trethevy is a dramatic example of a portal dolmen, one of the earliest forms of Neolithic burial chamber in Britain. Projecting side slabs created a shallow antechamber at the eastern end, where the capstone soars to over ten feet.

BOX 6099, ROHNERT PARK, CA 94927

Pomegranate

# SACRED STONES PHOTOGRAPHS BY
## MICK SHARP & JEAN WILLIAMSON

**Achavanich Stone Setting, Latheron, Caithness, Scotland.**
Thirty-six stones and stumps near Loch Stemster are still arranged
in an extremely rare long U-shaped setting open to the south.
More than fifty slabs were originally set at right angles to the
perimeter of the horseshoe. The nearby remains of a Neolithic
chamber and round cairn predate the Bronze Age setting.

BOX 6099, ROHNERT PARK, CA 94927

Pomegranate

# SACRED STONES PHOTOGRAPHS BY
## MICK SHARP & JEAN WILLIAMSON

### The Hurlers, Minions, Cornwall, England

Three stone circles in a line run up a slope on Bodmin Moor.
The Hurlers lie within sight of, and en route to, other ritual
monuments and distinctive granite outcrops, such as the
Cheesewring. Local legend describes the hammer-dressed
stones as a group of petrified men punished for "profaning
the Lord's Day with hurling the ball."

Pomegranate    BOX 6099, ROHNERT PARK, CA 94927

# SACRED STONES PHOTOGRAPHS BY
### MICK SHARP & JEAN WILLIAMSON

**Penrhos Feilw Standing Stones, Holyhead, Anglesey, Wales**
An unreliable nineteenth-century tradition places these schist
pillars at the center of a circle of smaller stones, as twin guardians
of a large burial cist containing arrowheads, spearheads, and bones.
The stones, ten feet high and eleven feet apart, were probably
erected as an isolated pair in the Bronze Age—that they catch
light from the setting sun seems purpose enough.

BOX 6099, ROHNERT PARK, CA 94927

Pomegranate

# SACRED STONES PHOTOGRAPHS BY
## MICK SHARP & JEAN WILLIAMSON

**St. Lythans Burial Chambers, Vale of Glamorgan, Wales**
All that remains of this Neolithic chambered cairn are the
megalithic burial chamber and faint traces of its long mound.
On the eastern end, the chamber faced into a recessed fore-
court that was sheltered by the cairn's projecting arms.

Pomegranate

BOX 6099, ROHNERT PARK, CA 94927

# SACRED STONES PHOTOGRAPHS BY
## MICK SHARP & JEAN WILLIAMSON

### Machrie Moor Stone Circle II, Arran, Scotland

Three sandstone slabs, weighing up to ten tons each, remain upright to a height of fifteen feet, while fragments of five others—including two crudely carved millstones—lie in the peat. Excavations in 1861 located a pair of cists, flint flakes, and a decorated Bronze Age pot within the circle.

BOX 6099, ROHNERT PARK, CA 94927

Pomegranate